W9-BZN-849

THE MIRACLE OF
THE HOLY
SPIRIT

Books by Charles L. Allen

Roads to Radiant Living
In Quest of God's Power
God's Psychiatry
When the Heart Is Hungry
The Touch of the Master's Hand
All Things Are Possible Through Prayer
When You Lose a Loved One
The Twenty-Third Psalm
Twelve Ways to Solve Your Problem
Healing Words
The Life of Christ
The Lord's Prayer
Prayer Changes Things
The Ten Commandments
The Sermon on the Mount
The Beatitudes
Life More Abundant
The Charles L. Allen Treasury
When You Graduate
The Miracle of Love
The Miracle of Hope
The Miracle of the Holy Spirit

231.3
P
276

THE MIRACLE OF THE HOLY SPIRIT

CHARLES L. ALLEN

FLEMING H. REVELL COMPANY
Old Tappan, New Jersey

Unless indicated otherwise, all Scripture quotations are from the King James Version of the Bible.

Scripture quotations identified RSV are from the Revised Standard Version of the Bible, Copyrighted 1946 and 1952.

Scripture quotations identified NEB are from *The New English Bible.* © The Delegates of the Oxford University Press and the Syndices of the Cambridge University Press 1961 and 1970. Reprinted by permission.

Excerpt from the hymn by John Greenleaf Whittier is from *The Complete Poetical Works of John Greenleaf Whittier* reprinted by permission of the publisher, Houghton Mifflin Company.

Excerpt by John Masefield is from "The Everlasting Mercy" from *Poems of John Masefield.* Copyright 1912 by Macmillan Publishing Company, Inc., renewed 1940 by John Masefield. Reprinted by permission.

Excerpt from *The Interpreter's Bible* is from INTERPRETER'S BIBLE, Vol. XI, page 213. Reprinted by permission of Abingdon Press.

Library of Congress Cataloging in Publication Data

Allen, Charles Livingstone, date
    The miracle of the Holy Spirit.

    1. Holy Spirit. I. Title.
BT121.2.A44   231'.3   74-10826
ISBN 0-8007-0688-9

Copyright © 1974 by Fleming H. Revell Company
All Rights Reserved
Printed in the United States of America

TO
Roy B. Sewell
Bremen, Georgia
A friend I appreciate and admire

Contents

Preface

This is the third in a series of small books on important themes of the Bible. The first was *The Miracle of Love*. The second was *The Miracle of Hope*. As I study the Bible, I always have several translations on my desk before me. Especially do I carefully read the *Revised Standard Version* and the *New English Bible*. However, for the most part, I quote the *King James Version*. This is the most familiar and many of us like best the lofty language of this version of the Bible.

In preparing this volume on the Holy Spirit, the temptation is to be lengthy. But I have purposely kept it brief and tried to put down the most essential facts.

Daily I have cause to thank God for the ministry He has given me through books. Every mail brings messages testifying that the reading of a book can be a blessing. This book is sent out with the prayer that those who read it will come to know intimately the blessed Holy Spirit.

I especially appreciate my dear wife, Leila, who gives me loving support. In the words of Solomon, "her price is far above rubies." Mrs. Constance Ward carefully typed this manuscript and I appreciate her efforts.

CHARLES L. ALLEN

The grace of the Lord Jesus Christ, and the love of God, and the fellowship of the Holy Spirit be with you all.

2 Corinthians 13:14 RSV

1

The Promise of the Coming of the Holy Spirit

I love preliminary things—
The tuning up of flutes and strings,
The little scrolls musicians play,
The varying keys to feel their way,
The hum—the hush in which it dies,
But most to see the curtain rise.

HALFORD E. LUCCOCK

The fourteenth chapter of Saint John's Gospel sees the curtain falling on one drama but rising on another. Jesus is saying to His closest friends that soon He will be physically present with them no more. They are visibly disturbed. He says to them, "Let not your heart be troubled" (*see* John 14:1). He is not saying, "Do not feel sorrow." Here on this earth we come to love each other more than we love ourselves. Then this experience we call death comes to some loved one. It brings deep and abiding sorrow to our hearts.

After I had conducted a funeral service for a lovely young girl, her mother said to me, "How long will it take me to get over this?" I asked, "Do you really want to ever get over it?" She replied, "No." We do not get over our sorrows. Sorrows become permanent and precious possessions of our hearts.

To His loved ones, Jesus is saying, "Do not be worried—disturbed." He assures them that death is not the end of life. He says,

"In my Father's house. . . . I go to prepare a place for you. . . . Because I live, ye shall live also" (John 14:1, 2, 19). He gives them assurance that His life is not ending and neither will their own lives end with death.

To be with Christ in the flesh was for these men a glorious experience. How inspired they felt in His presence! They carefully listened as He told those simple stories. They would never forget the story of the father who had two sons, or the Samaritan who helped the wounded man, or the farmer who found the buried treasure in the field, or any of the others. They saw marvelous miracles which He wrought. The eyes of blind people were opened, cripples were made to walk, winds and waves obeyed His voice. But soon He would be with them no more. It had been such a short time —less than three years. They had expected the Lord to establish His Kingdom on earth and they saw no signs of it. Not only the sorrow of His leaving—loneliness, disappointment, and defeat began to settle upon them. To those disciples the curtain truly was falling.

> **And I will pray the Father, and he shall give you another Comforter, that he may abide with you for ever.**
>
> **John 14:16**

Jesus lifted the curtain on an entirely new drama. For generations the people of Israel had looked for the coming of the Christ. Then came that night when an angel of the Lord announced, "For unto you is born this day in the city of David a Saviour, which is Christ the Lord" (Luke 2:11). He lived among them and He accomplished His purpose. Now it was time for the days of His flesh on earth to end. But He was not leaving them alone.

The Father shall give them another **Comforter**, Jesus promised. For us today, that word "Comforter," as the King James Version uses it, is not adequate. It merely has some such meaning as sympathy in time of sorrow. Truly, none gives such comfort as the Holy Spirit, as at times when we sing Paul Gerhardt's hymn, which begins, "Holy Ghost, dispel our sadness; Pierce the clouds of nature's night."

The *Revised Standard Version* uses the word "Counselor," but neither is that word adequate. One of our favorite hymns is Samuel Longfellow's, "Holy Spirit, Truth Divine," in which he bids the Spirit to "Wake my spirit, clear my sight." The Spirit does cause us to see clearer, and to understand more fully.

Other translators use such words as *Advocate, Helper, Intercessor, Teacher.* All of these and many other words apply to the purpose and work of the Holy Spirit. But I think the best translation of what Jesus said is simply, "And he shall give you another **person.**" When Jesus came, He came as a person. Even though the Holy Spirit does not have a physical body, He is no less a person.

Right at this point we see a dramatic difference between the Old and New Testaments. In the Old Testament, the Spirit of God is a power which acts in the material universe to sustain the physical life of man. It is an impersonal power. In the earlier pages of the New Testament, the Spirit of God is still presented as this impersonal power. In the very beginning of the Creation story, we are told, ". . . . the Spirit of God moved upon the face of the waters" (Genesis 1:2).

To the Hebrews, God was completely apart from the world. He was way off someplace, but could and would send a spiritual force to do things on the earth. This force or Spirit of God could not be escaped from. "Whither shall I go from thy spirit? or whither shall I flee from thy presence?" cries the psalmist (Psalms 139:7). Man was dependent on the Spirit for life—"And the Lord said, My spirit shall not always strive with man: . . . yet his days shall be a hundred and twenty years" (Genesis 6:3). It was the Spirit which kept men physically alive.

Exceptional physical power was attributed to the Spirit of God. For example, when Samson was attacked by a lion, we read, "And the Spirit of the Lord came mightily upon him, and he rent him as he would have rent a kid . . ." (Judges 14:6). We read how the Spirit of God gave Saul the power to inflict terrible chastisement in battle on the Ammonites (*see* 1 Samuel 11:6–11).

There are many references in the Old Testament as to how the Spirit of God directed the prophets and gave them visions. Zechariah speaks of ". . . the words which the Lord of hosts hath sent in his Spirit by the former prophets" (*see* Zechariah 7:12). The Spirit gave to the prophets earthly wisdom. But as we study the work of the Spirit in the Old Testament, we see that its work is almost never directed toward the spiritual development of the person.

When David prays, ". . . take not thy holy spirit from me" (Psalms 51:11), it seems clear he believes God's Spirit is essential for the well-being of his own soul. But this is a very rare thought in the Old Testament. To the psalmist and prophets, God's Spirit was a power.

In contrast, Jesus made clear to His disciples that a person would come and be with them, just as He had been with them. In association with Jesus, the disciples had been comforted, taught and inspired. Likewise would they be by the Holy Spirit. The Spirit would teach them and keep their memories refreshed of Christ and what He had taught them (*see* John 14:26). The Spirit would be their personal companion. The work of redeeming men which God began through His Son, would be carried on by the Father through the Holy Spirit. "And when he is come, he will reprove the world of sin, and of righteousness, and of judgment" (John 16:8).

. . . **It is expedient for you that I go away.** . . .

John 16:7

How could it be expedient—or profitable—or to their good, that Jesus go away? It seemed they would lose everything in His leaving

—the joy of His Presence, the blessing of His words, the inspiration of His example, the reality of His leadership. It is true that He promised that in His stead would come the Spirit, but that was so vague. How could a Spirit take the place of a person? Even today we long for Jesus' physical presence. We sing:

> I think when I read that sweet story of old,
> When Jesus was here among men,
> How He called little children as lambs to His fold—
> I should like to have been with them then.
>
> I wish that His hands had been placed on my head,
> That His arms had been thrown around me,
> And that I might have seen His kind look when He said,
> "Let the little ones come unto Me."

JEMIMA T. LUKE

One of the strong appeals of the Second Coming of Christ for many people is right at this point. Many still think of the Holy Spirit as a gracious, divine influence but not as a living person. Many people profoundly believe that if Christ were here again in the flesh, then all the problems of this world would be solved. To begin with, even if Christ were here in the flesh today, we have no assurance that any more people would recognize Him as the Son of God than did when He was here. But even if He would be recognized by all people, not very many people could be physically close to Him. Some people who had the money could journey to where He was. He could preach to crowds of people. Today He could even be on worldwide television, but that would not satisfy the longing to have His hands "placed on my head."

His being here today in the flesh presents even greater difficulty. Those who believe in Him would expect Him to make every decision and we might become mere puppets. Today we ask, "What would Christ do?" but the answer to that question requires our own thinking. If He were here in body, we would not have to think. Even worse to consider, if Christ were here today in body, it is very possible that He would be crucified again. After nearly two thousand years, we have still not fully understood, and certainly not fully lived by, the words He spoke when He was here in the flesh. We likely would not accept His words any more completely if we actually heard them from His lips. To His disciples He said, "I have yet many things to say unto you, but ye cannot bear them now" (John 16:12). We have no real reason to believe we could today bear the things He would say.

It is so much better that Christ lives in my heart than it would be for Him to live in the flesh in my city—or maybe in some city on the other side of the world. To His disciples He said, "But because I have said these things unto you, sorrow hath filled your heart" (John 16:6). The reason for their sorrow was that at that time they could not at all understand that another person would come in His place. In spite of the whole record since, many people today still do not understand. For many the Holy Spirit is still vague and impersonal.

Here let us emphasize again that the Holy Spirit is a person. In the sports pages of the newspaper we read about the spirit of the football team. We remember the spirit of our school when we were there. A man spoke to me recently about the friendly spirit of his church. But in none of these cases, or in many others which might come to mind, is this spirit to be compared to a person.

Many people today, even though they think of themselves as devout Christians, have no real sense of an actual Presence. To many, God is real, except He is far away. He lives "up yonder somewhere" completely aloof from all the everyday happenings on this earth. A group of people were asked if God understood modern computers and a goodly number thought He did not. They think of God as a sort of grandfather, kind and loving, but not really a part of things today. Some think of Him as Almighty God, but so Almighty that He has no time for earthly matters which concern us.

To many, Christ is simply somebody who lived on this earth nearly two centuries ago. To these the Christian faith consists mainly of studying the record of His earthly life. It embraced a period of about thirty-three years and that is it! It is good to study what He said and did, to believe that He set in motion some lovely ideals, but now He sits on a throne in heaven at the right hand of God. Many do not think of Christ as being a part of life today. One can think of great, inspiring heroes of the past—Moses, David, Saint Paul, Augustine, Luther, Wesley—and so many others. Their lives continue to be an inspiration to us now. One would hardly say, "O Martin Luther, come and help me now." Tragically, many feel that way about Christ. They are merely believing in a Christ who once lived—period.

". . . It is expedient that I go away." Then Jesus goes on to say, "for if I go not away, the Comforter will not come unto you; but if I depart, I will send him unto you" (John 16:7).

Dr. Russell Mattby in his book *The Meaning of the Resurrection,* says:

> When he had finished that which he came to do and had shown himself so that we knew him, it was expedient for us that he should go back out of the here into the everywhere, out of some men's sight that he might be near to all men's hearts.

> **And when he comes, he will convince the world of sin and of righteousness and of judgment. He will glorify me. . . .**

> **John 16: 8, 14** RSV

Speaking of the work of the Holy Spirit, Christ says first it is to convince the world of *sin.* The Christian faith is more—much more —than a beautiful system of ethics, or a guide for life, or even a revelation of truth. It is a redemptive power from sin. Man does not like to face the reality of sin and until one believes that sin is sin, he will feel no need of a Saviour. We humans are quick to confess our physical weaknesses or psychological complexes, and thereby excuse ourselves for our transgressions. But the Holy Spirit will convince man that sin is against God and that "the wages of sin is death" (*see* Romans 6:23).

Next comes convincing of *righteousness*. Man cannot be convinced of righteousness until first he is convinced of sin. Healing has no appeal to one who does not know he is sick. There is no point in offering salvation to one who does not believe himself to be lost. Preaching the love of God makes no impression on one who does not realize he is separated from God through sin. The Holy Spirit convinces man of his need for the righteousness which God provides and makes available.

"And of judgment." The fact of sin and the fact of righteousness result in the fact of *judgment*. Sin and righteousness are constantly striving for dominion over man. Judgment is involved in man's every choice, word, and act. Not only is judgment day by day, there is also *the Judgment*.

Just to become convinced of sin, righteousness and judgment would be to make man hopelessly miserable. Man can neither save himself from sin nor achieve righteousness. This is why God sent His Son in the first place. "He that believeth on Him is not condemned . . ." (John 3:18). So Christ tells His disciples and us, "He will glorify me" (*see* John 16:14 RSV).

It is a wonder of wonders that Christ was not forgotten long ago. He lived a very short number of years in a time when there were no photographs or printed books. He never sought publicity for Himself and again and again after some miracle He would say, "Tell no man." He died between two thieves and even His Resurrection was quiet and unobtrusive. There were no blinding flashes of lightning to compel man to believe. After His Resurrection, He very gently talked with a very few people. Every day He is denied by countless hearts. Why has He not passed into oblivion? Because the Holy Spirit works within the heart of man. Christ now works with man, not from without through physical contact, but from within by His indwelling Presence. He is not a person walking on earth in the flesh. He is now a person living in the hearts of people.

Christ is glorified through the ministry of the Holy Spirit, also, by a fuller understanding of Him. The disciples had been so close to Him, so busy with much coming and going, so overwhelmed by His works, so caught up in their selfish desires for Him to establish an earthly Kingdom, that they had missed much of His divine significance.

For example, we know and understand Abraham Lincoln better today than men did a hundred years ago. During his lifetime, Lincoln was misunderstood by so many. The large conflicts in ideas and in war swirled about the man to obscure him. But as the years have passed, we have better caught his spirit and understood his character. We have had this experience with our own loved ones whom we may have lost for a while. Many of us feel we know our parents better now than we did when we were living together in the same house. Had Jesus lived physically as long as the disciples lived, they would never have understood Him. If He were living today on earth in the flesh, we would not understand Him nearly as well as we do. The Holy Spirit glorifies Christ by revealing Him to man.

Charles Wesley expressed it in the second verse of his hymn, "Spirit of Faith, Come Down."

> No man can truly say
> That Jesus is the Lord,
> Unless Thou take the veil away,
> And breathe the Living Word.

. . . lo, I am with you alway. . . .

Matthew 28:20

What strange words to come from Christ's lips at that moment! He knew that He would be ascending into heaven that very day.

He had left them once before when He went to the grave, but that time He knew He would be back with them here on this earth. He would only be away three days and then He would be resurrected. This time it was different. He had told them that "Hereafter shall the Son of man sit on the right hand of the power of God" (Luke 22:69). He would never be with them again as He had been—yet He said, "I will be with you alway."

The disciples had become convinced that Jesus survived death. He convinced them through their physical senses—they saw Him through their own eyes, they touched Him with their own hands, they heard His voice through their own ears. In this connection, there are two notable differences in His relationship with His followers before and after the Resurrection. First, He seemed to want to use the physical senses no more than was necessary. Second, He made unexpected appearances and disappearances. He wanted them to know His Presence at all times without the physical. He was, in fact, preparing them for the ministry of the Holy Spirit.

Mary Magdalene sat weeping in the garden. She saw someone who she supposed was a gardener until He spoke her name. Then she knew it was the Lord. She was overcome with joy and likely made as if to fall at His feet but Jesus said, "Touch me not." He had already used some of the physical senses, and did not want to use more of the senses than necessary. He wanted to lead her and all His followers forever afterward to the point at which they did not need the physical senses to believe in His Presence (*see* John 20:11-18).

Two of His friends were walking home to Emmaus from Jerusalem. Jesus fell in step with them but was unrecognized. As they walked together He ". . . explained to them the passages which referred to himself in every part of the scriptures" (Luke 24:27 NEB). They were comforted and inspired. Here Christ was fulfilling one of the functions of the Holy Spirit in teaching and instructing. He entered their house and sat at the table. As He broke the bread they recognized Him and He immediately disappeared (*see* Luke 24:30, 31).

As the disciples were gathered together in an upper room He suddenly appeared in their midst (John 20:19-23). One morning as some of the disciples came in from fishing, they saw Him on the shore (John 21:4).

Surely Mary would never sit in a garden again without knowing her Rabboni was there. Those dear friends in Emmaus forever afterward set a place for the unseen Lord at their table. The disciples would take account of His Presence in every gathering of theirs from then on. Peter and the others would be sure Jesus was there every time they walked on the shores of Lake Galilee. The lesson was learned—the Presence of Christ did not have to be physical. They—and countless others since that day—could sing the hymn which begins:

> Be present at our table, Lord;
> Be here and ev'rywhere adored;
>
> JOHN CENNICK

and the words do not seem strange.

. . . He was parted from them, and carried up into heaven.

Luke 24:51

This is the Ascension. Jesus and His disciples went out of the city as far as Bethany. There He lifted His hands and during the act of blessing them, "He was parted from them, and carried into heaven." Notice the difference in their reaction to this parting and the one just a few weeks before when they saw Him buried. This time there was no fear, no sorrow, no frustration.

One might expect to read that, after Christ's disappearance, "The disciples returned to Jerusalem with tears blinding their eyes," or "with broken hearts at their parting," or with the feeling it was good to be with Him but now it was all over. Instead, Luke concludes his Gospel with the words "And they . . . returned to

Jerusalem with great joy: And [they] were continually in the temple, praising and blessing God. Amen" (Luke 24:52, 53).

They never thought of Jesus again as being dead. They picked no flowers for a grave. They wrote no memorial verses. They erected no monuments to Him. In truth, they never **remembered** Him because they never thought of Him as belonging to the past. The people who only believe in a Christ who once lived in Galilee have missed the point. For the disciples, the Ascension was in no sense good-by. In no way did they feel they had lost their Lord. Their faith was made firm and fully vindicated.

There are so many lessons to be learned from our Lord's Ascension that space here does not permit me to discuss, but I must briefly mention two. One is in reference to the suffering which mankind is made to bear—and there is so much of it. Often we talk about how God allowed His Son to suffer on the Cross. But we must not stop with suffering. We must not forget the words in the Apostles' Creed, ". . . the third day He rose again from the dead; He ascended into heaven." Death is not the end. Love is never defeated. All the question marks in life are eventually erased.

A second thought—I was trying as best I could to ease the anguish of a young mother after we had buried her precious baby. I talked about how God had provided her with arms to hold that little one. That baby was born into this world with somebody to love it. We talked about how little children ran to the arms of Jesus. Now He is in heaven and He is no less there than He was here. There is real truth in the gospel song, "Safe in the Arms of Jesus."

. . . tarry ye in the city of Jerusalem. . . .

Luke 24:49

Before His Ascension, Christ said to His disciples, "And, behold, I send the promise of my Father upon you: but tarry ye in the city of Jerusalem, until ye be endued with power from on high."

Many preachers have told the story about Jesus meeting an angel when He ascended back into heaven. The angel inquired as to what plans He had made for the carrying on of His work on earth. Jesus replied that He had charged His disciples to "Go ye into all the world, and preach the gospel to every creature" (Mark 16:15). The angel asked, "But suppose they fail, what other plans did you make?" Jesus replied, "I made no other plans." We tell that story to illustrate His faith in them and in us. But that story is not really adequate. There was more than just His faith in human beings. The final plan was the coming and ministry of the Holy Spirit.

Jesus never expected the Kingdom of God to be established on earth just by people like us. He knew that He had taught these disciples, He had shown them miracles, He had established a sense of His Presence. There had to be more—they had to have a power which they had not yet received.

There are many Christian people today who are still in Bethany, from whence the Lord ascended. They believe that Jesus was the Son of God. They have studied the words that fell from His lips —the Sermon on the Mount, the parables of the good Samaritan and the prodigal son and the others. They believe that He walked on the water and healed the sick. They have come to love Him and endeavor to obey His commandments. But that is not enough. These first disciples knew Christ on earth, yet they were lacking in power, and that night in Gethsemane one of them denied Him and the others "forsook Him, and fled" (*see* Matthew 26:56).

There are other Christians today who call Jesus *Lord and Master*. They believe He is the Saviour of the world. They have learned that He died for the sins of men, that He rose from the grave and is now ascended to the Father. They believe that when they are gathered together in His name that His Presence is among them. They think that is all there is. If that had been enough, then Jesus would have told the disciples to begin preaching there in Bethany. There would have been no need to go back and tarry in Jerusalem.

There are other Christians who have gone from Bethany to that upper room in Jerusalem, but they are still sitting there. They are waiting, praying and longing for the coming of the Holy Spirit. They do not realize that the Spirit did come, that the Spirit has never left, and there is no reason for Him to come again. They do not know that the Spirit abides with us forever.

> **But ye shall receive power, after that the Holy [Spirit] is come upon you: and ye shall be witnesses unto me. . . .**
>
> Acts 1:8

One cannot be a witness **for** something until he has been a witness **to** something. Sometime ago I served on a jury in court. The case involved an automobile accident. A man was seated on the witness stand and the attorney asked him, "Did you see the accident?" The man replied that he did. Then the attorney said, "Tell us about it." But if the man had not seen the accident, then he would never have been asked to tell about it.

It is important to note that the words "witness" and "martyr" come from the same Greek word *martus*. When Jesus says to His disciples "ye shall be witnesses unto me," He literally means that when they have truly experienced the coming of the Holy Spirit, then they will be willing to tell the world about it, even though it means their own death. It means that after the Holy Spirit has come upon them, they will have the power to testify even at the cost of their own lives. No fear could then hold them back. No wonder they could turn the world upside down!

When the church today is baptized with the Holy Spirit, no power on the earth can stop it. Without the Spirit, the church has no effective witness.

2

The Coming of the Holy Spirit

... they went up into an upper room. ...

Acts 1:13

It was on Thursday that the disciples returned to Jerusalem, probably late in the afternoon. Luke tells us they "were continually in the temple, praising and blessing God" (Luke 24:53). Likely they went there first. Often they had been there to worship but never before with such joy in their hearts. They did not go to the temple for a memorial service for the Lord. There was no sign of mourning about them. They knew the joy of triumph—triumph already accomplished and the triumph to come, as promised.

From the temple they went to an *upper room*. Maybe it was the room in which had occurred the Last Supper. It might have been in the house of Mary, the mother of Mark. The eleven disciples were there, only Judas was missing. Some women joined their number, including Mary the mother of Jesus. Also, among them were Jesus' brothers. Others came. All together there gathered about a hundred and twenty (*see* Acts 1:13–15).

"These all continued with one accord in prayer and supplication . . ." (Acts 1:14). Now they were united—*one accord*. Their selfish ambitions and jealousies of each other were gone. They had all been caught up in a vision and a purpose greater than themselves. They had "lost their lives for Christ's sake."

This night prayer was a much more real experience than they had ever known before. They were not praying to some unknown, unreal God. Their own Christ was now with the Father. They surely remembered Jesus saying, "Whatsoever ye shall ask the Father in my name, he will give it to you" (John 16:23). For the very first time, prayers were sent to Heaven's throne which were authorized and accredited by the name of God's only begotten Son.

Maybe Martha was in the upper room that night. If so, she doubtless remembered that dark day when she met the Lord on the road after the death of her brother Lazarus. Even then she still had faith as she said, ". . . even now, whatsoever thou wilt ask of God, God will give it thee" (John 11:22). Knowing that Jesus was now sitting at the right hand of God, she and every other Christian could pray with new faith and confidence.

So that Thursday night, they joyously prayed for the coming of the Holy Spirit. It was on Thursday night that they had eaten the Last Supper and it was on Thursday night that Jesus had prayed in Gethsemane. This would be the night. But midnight came and nothing had happened.

Finally came the dawn of Friday morning. This was the day the Lord had died. Surely He would send the Comforter today. All day long they remembered the Cross and every detail of His death. Toward dusk they likely talked about His burial and their own loneliness and fear that day. Yet Friday passed and still no "baptism of fire."

Perhaps they did not expect anything to happen on Saturday but they continued in prayer, knowing that next would come the first day of the week—the day of the Resurrection. He had said, ". . . ye shall be baptized with the Holy [Spirit] not many days hence" (Acts 1:5). This was the fourth day. Sunday is to the week what Easter is to the year. But still He did not come.

Monday, Tuesday, Wednesday came and went. So did Thursday, Friday and Saturday. For ten days they had been praying and nothing had happened. Jesus had told them, "Tarry ye in the city of Jerusalem, until. . . ." (*see* Luke 24:49). But ten days seemed so long. They would go out for a bite to eat or for some other necessary routine, but would hurry back. No one wanted to be absent when **that moment** came. Doubtless they encouraged each other as they would repeat Jesus' words—"But ye shall receive power, after that the Holy [Spirit] is come upon you . . ." (Acts 1:8). "Tarry until ye be endued with power from on high" (*see* Luke 24:49). ". . . Ye shall be witnesses unto me . . . unto the uttermost part of the earth" (Acts 1:8). Because they believed what the Lord said, they could keep on waiting and praying, and praying and waiting.

But is there a limit to how much waiting a person can stand? Many have found waiting to be very hard. There is great anticipation in a prayer being answered but prolonged waiting can wear one's spirit down. Waiting too long can pour cold water on the fire of enthusiasm. Do we suppose that they began to feel that maybe they were not worthy for the Spirit to come upon them? James could remind himself of his ambition for the chief seat. Thomas could remember his doubts. Peter could remember his denial. Each one of them assembled there could remember failing to stand up for Him in His trials, and even failing to comfort Him as He died.

Even in this enlightened day, there are Christians who blame themselves when some prayer is not instantly answered. Many have prayed for a season but gave up in self-condemnation when the waiting seemed long. Or worse, instead of self-condemnation, some give up in God-condemnation. Do we suppose that someone in that upper room might have said, " 'Not many days,' He promised, but the promise has been broken." We do not think anyone in that room lost faith, but we know that at times the lamp of our own faith has flickered. Can one really believe God's promises? That question has burned in many tortured minds.

"Why does the Lord delay?" they must have wondered. The Gospel needs to be preached. The earth needs to hear the trumpet sound. There are so many who are lost in sin. Jesus died that repentance and remission of sins should be preached. Multitudes are sick who need to be helped. Daily, people are dying in unbelief. "Why should we tarry longer?" they might have said. He had instructed them and He had commissioned them. Surely it was time to go.

Impatience is one of life's heaviest burdens to bear. We all feel that burden at times. Waiting can be a dreary experience. Many of us have found it so. But let it be said to the credit of every one of those one hundred and twenty people who were praying in the upper room, not one of them quit. Every one of them abided by His words, "Tarry ye . . . until." **Until** is a word to be underscored!

And when the day of Pentecost was fully come. . . .

Acts 2:1

Pentecost came on an important day in Jewish history. We recall how the blood of the lamb was put upon the door of the people of Israel when they were in captivity, which averted death from their houses. Fifty days afterwards they reached the mountain where God manifested Himself and the people realized that truly the captivity was broken. For generations they had celebrated this day. In the Old Testament this celebration was called by several names; the Feast of Harvest; the Feast of Weeks; the Feast of First Fruits. This celebration commemorated the giving of the Law on Mount Sinai. It was their custom to read publicly in the synagogues during this period the account of the giving of the Law in Exodus, the first chapter of Ezekiel, and the third chapter of Habakkuk.

Forty days Jesus had been with them since His Resurrection. Ten days He had been out of their sight. Now on the fiftieth day, Pentecost came. It marked the beginning of a new era in God's relations with mankind. God's revelation on Mount Sinai was accompanied by fire, noises, and voices (*see* Exodus 19:16–19). Likewise was the coming of the Holy Spirit so marked. Just as the people remembered how they were delivered from bondage and their entrance into the promised land, henceforth would Christians remember this day as the fulfillment of Christ's promises of the coming of the Comforter and their enduement with power for the work to which they had been appointed. From this day on they would never fear defeat because the Holy Spirit would be with them.

Pentecost is the birthday of the Christian church. This is the day on which the Christians really began their triumphant mission in the world, which mission will never cease until all the earth is conquered for Christ. Because of Pentecost, the Christian knows that the words of our Lord's Prayer, "Thy kingdom come on earth," will one day be fully accomplished.

> **. . . the number of names together were about an hundred and twenty.**
>
> **Acts 1:15**

It is of extreme importance to note the fact that Pentecost came when they were assembled together. Throughout the history of the church, coming together has been of the utmost importance. This is why we build places of worship. There are those who have condemned the spending of money on church buildings, but without a place to come together, the church would soon die. We read in *The Interpreter's Bible:*

> D.L. Moody once called on a leading citizen in Chicago to persuade him to accept Christ. They were seated in the man's parlor. It was winter and coal was burning in the fireplace. The man objected that he could be just as good a Christian outside the church as in it. Moody said nothing, but stepped to the fireplace, took the tongs, picked a blazing coal from the fire and set it off by itself. In silence the two watched it smolder and go out. "I see," said the man.

The author of Hebrews tells us, "And let us consider one another to provoke unto love and to good works: Not forsaking the assembling of ourselves together . . ." (Hebrews 10:24, 25).

Much of the excitement at a football game is because of the crowd. Even the most exciting game would be pretty dull if you were alone in the stands or if just a few were scattered over the seats. We catch enthusiasm from each other. Likewise in God's House. A full church generates enthusiasm for God. The assembling together does inspire us to love and good works.

I am the pastor of a church which has almost eleven thousand members. The church roll is contained in a large cabinet in the church office. Sometimes I stand before that cabinet and I get very excited. I think of all the names listed as members and I think about what would happen if all those people came to church every Sunday. What a thrilling witness it would be! What a power the church would become! Suppose all eleven thousand came! I think of how one hundred and twenty went out from Pentecost to turn the world upside down.

The greatest disappointment of any pastor is the fact that so many of the church members fail to attend the services in the church. There is a group which calls itself Seventh-day Adventists. But the largest group in the Christian church today is the Seventh-day **Absentists.** The absent members on the Lord's Day are the shame of every church. Pentecost would never have come had they not been assembled together.

We read, "For he [Judas] was numbered with us . . ." (Acts 1:17). There is tragedy in those words. Here was a man who used to belong. His name was on the roll, but he was no longer a member. Of course, Judas was now dead, but today there are many names on every church roll who are not active members. This points up one of the first responsibilities of the church. Through the years the church has emphasized evangelism and that is good. It is our business to win others to faith in Christ. It is no less our business in the church to win back those who are numbered with us but who do not come anymore.

Some of the happiest experiences I have had as a pastor are right at this point. I will use space here to cite only one example. Some years ago I received a Negro family into the church. They were the first black people this church had received as members. It caused some unhappiness among a goodly number of the members. One man wrote me a bitter letter stating that he would never enter the church again and demanding that his name be taken off the roll. It would have been easy to have condemned that man for his prejudice, to have called him unchristian, and to have said that removing his name was a good riddance. Instead, I visited with him in his home several times. As we talked and prayed together, gradually the fires of resentment in his heart died down. He did come back to the church and today he is numbered among us as a faithful member. It is just as important to keep a member as it is to win a new member, and it is just as incumbent upon us who are in the church.

In one place brings to mind another thought. God gives to each one He calls a place of service. There are different places for different people, but important for each is to ask, "What is my place in God's work?" As we serve faithfully in our own place, we find we have opportunity, ability and power to do that work. I like to paraphrase Psalms 91:1 to read, "He who occupies the place of the Lord's appointment will be conscious of the presence and power of the Almighty."

These all continued . . . in prayer and supplication with . . . Mary the mother of Jesus. . . .

Acts 1:14

Mary was with them as they were gathered together in that upper room. Her presence there is beautiful. As we see her there, our minds go back to that pure young girl to whom the angel said, "And, behold, thou shalt conceive in thy womb, and bring forth a son, and shalt call his name Jesus" (Luke 1:31). What a glorious thing to be so selected by God and how happy she was when He was born. We think of those years together in Nazareth as He grew up. She gave to Him all that a mother could give. She knew He was God's own Son. She believed in His mission and she never doubted.

Then came those terrible experiences—the betrayal by one of His own disciples—the soldiers taking Him—the shameful trials—the denial of Peter—the march up Calvary bearing a Cross—the agony of His Crucifixion—His death and burial. One wonders how Mary could have even survived through it all. She not only experienced deep sorrow but also bitter disappointment. It would have been so easy for her to have felt deserted by God. She might have refused to ever trust God again. She might have said that she would never go back to church. But there she was praying with the others in that upper room.

Hers is a wonderful example of how life can go on even with a broken heart. So often grief is used as an excuse for withdrawal. A deep sorrow can become a paralyzing hand upon a person's life. Mary might have never been heard of again. So often a person's life *does* stop at the point where great loss or deep hurt has occurred. But Mary shows us a more excellent way. Here she was quietly taking her place among the others. She demanded no special consideration. She was willing to be one among the hundred and twenty, doing what she could.

The remaining pages of this volume could be devoted to this point. Countless numbers among us have experienced sorrows that made it hard for us to go on. I remember well the difficulty I had in preaching the next Sunday after we had buried our first grandson. As a pastor I have been sympathetic with so many. Through years of experience I have learned to say to people several things:

(1) Your sorrow admits you into a very large fellowship. There are many, many others who have walked through a similar valley. Do not think you are the only one to whom this has happened.

(2) It is normal and right to feel sorrow—do not be ashamed of your tears. Some unknown writer exclaimed: "The soul would have no rainbow had the eyes no tears." But remember that the excessive expression of grief is not a method of showing love, as some seem to think.

(3) Be careful not to slip into self-pity. After sorrow there is temptation to feel sorry for ourselves and that can become a growing and devastating experience. There are some people and there are proper times to share our sorrows, but continually talking about them with everyone who will listen makes them worse. The more you complain, the more you have to complain about.

(4) Don't surrender to your sorrow. In one of Ibsen's plays, one of the characters asks another, "Who taught thee to sing?" The answer is: "God sent me a sorrow."

Mary was there—praying with the others!

. . . they were all with one accord. . . .

Acts 2:1

One accord does not mean agreement on every subject. Certainly there is room for differences of opinion among Christians. For example, in a political election some may vote for one candidate and some for another. The important thing is that we recognize that each has the freedom to decide for himself and, even though one has a different view from another, Christians continue to love and believe in each other despite those differences. "One accord" does not mean complete conformity in all matters. Within the Christian fellowship there is ample room for a variety of opinions and ideas.

Some have felt that the existence of many denominations within the Christian faith is wrong and that we should all be united in one communion.

In his book *The Power of Faith,* Louis Binstock tells how David Starr Jordan described the search for the infinite as a mountain climb. Separate bands of people are struggling up the steep slopes, desperately straining to reach the summit. Each group has chosen its own path; it is certain that it alone travels the right one; is calling to the others: "Come with us. We'll show you the way. We have found the real road." The truth is that from the vantage point of the mountaintop, where only God has a panoramic view of the climbers below, all the paths lead to the summit. All the bands can attain the coveted objective, if they continue climbing upward instead of diverting themselves with petty pleasures and costly conflicts that constantly drag them downward. They need not join each other on the way up. Nonetheless, they will someday find themselves standing at the highest peaks together, if they never stop their search after God.

What is important to know is that these first Christians were in *one accord* with the commission they had received from the Lord. They were all committed to witness when they had been endued with God's power. Each one was not only counted among the group, but was saying, "Count on me." In our churches today there are members who are counted but cannot be counted on.

When Christian people are of one accord, they might pray as did the founder of the Society of Jesus in "Prayer for Generosity."

> Teach us, good Lord, to serve Thee
>   as Thou deservest;
> To give and not to count the cost;
> To fight and not to heed the wounds;
> To toil and not to seek for rest;

> To labor and not to ask for any reward
> Save that of knowing that we do Thy will;
> Through Jesus Christ our Lord.

ST. IGNATIUS LOYOLA

John Wesley also expressed this personal commitment.

> Is thy heart right, as my heart is with thine?
> Dost thou love and serve God? It is enough.
> I give thee the right hand of fellowship.

The power of God never comes upon one who is not first committed to God's purpose. Becoming committed, one becomes convinced the power will come. That is why they could keep on praying and waiting. Committed churchpeople see the power of God, but uncommitted churchpeople see only the problems of the world.

And suddenly there came a sound from heaven as of a rushing mighty wind, and it filled all the house where they were sitting.

Acts 2:2

Actually no wind occurred. The house in which they were was not shaken, neither did a storm or gale sweep across the city. No one felt any movement of air. Instead, there was a sound of wind. They heard it but did not see or feel the wind blowing. The disciples had weathered many storms at sea and they had heard "rushing mighty winds" many times. What they heard was that same sound but this sound came out of a clear sky. There were no naturalistic grounds by which it would be explained. They were sure of one thing—it came *from heaven.*

Here we have reenacted the great miracle in chapter 37 of

Ezekiel. The prophet saw great numbers of bones lying on the ground in the valley. These bones were dry, dead and decaying. There was no life in them. The Lord said to Ezekiel, "Can these bones live?" He replied to God, "Thou knowest" (*see* verses 1–3). Then God commanded the prophet to tell the bones that God would cause breath to enter them; that they would live; that they would take on flesh and skin (*see* verses 4–6).

The bones then became covered with flesh and skin, and they came together, "bone to his bone." But still they were dead. Then God told Ezekiel to say to the wind, "Come from the four winds, O breath, and breathe upon these slain that they may live" (*see* verses 7–9). When the wind blew, we read, "Breath came into them, and they lived, and stood upon their feet, an exceeding great army" (*see* verse 10).

This is what happened at Pentecost. These people had physical life but they were spiritually dead and powerless. Then came God's breath upon them—breath that was life-giving. The result was that they immediately had the courage to stand on their own feet. From that moment it could rightly be said, "Like a mighty army moves the church of God." What happened is what John speaks of, "Ye have an unction from the Holy One" (*see* 1 John 2:20). The *Revised Standard Version* uses the word "anointed." The *New English Bible* uses the word "initiated." But for many of us the word "unction" says it better. I can remember many years ago, after a preacher had preached an unusually moving sermon, people would say, "He had unction from on high." That is what they got that day in that upper room.

Since that day of Pentecost, the breath of God has continued to descend upon God's men and God's world. This energy faced the paganism of the ancient world and brought it to the dust. As it has passed over civilization, it has caused flowers to grow just like a rain causes a desert to bloom. When this breath of God comes into a human heart, one has a new power—a power that makes him both strong and good. I have a little sailboat in which I sometimes go out on the Gulf of Mexico. When the wind is still, the sails hang limp and the little boat can only drift with the tide. But when the wind comes and fills the sails, the boat moves and goes somewhere, even against the tide. When the *wind of God* fills the soul of a person, that person becomes possessed by a purpose and has the power to move toward the accomplishment of that purpose. This is power—the power of the Holy Spirit in the life of man.

And so we sing:

> Breathe on me, Breath of God,
> Fill me with life anew,
> That I may love what Thou dost love,
> And do what Thou wouldst do.

EDWIN HATCH

Here we have the fulfilling of the promise, "But ye shall receive power, after that the Holy [Spirit] is come upon you . . ." (Acts 1:8). Notice it was the sound of a "mighty wind." *Weymouth* translates it "a blast"; and *Moffatt* uses the words, "a violent blast." The *New English Bible* says, "a strong driving wind." Nowhere is it called "a gentle breeze."

On this day a new word was introduced into the Christian vocabulary—it was the word **power.** After this the word *power* is used more than fifty times in the New Testament. It is of great importance to the Christian to have the assurance that God's power is both real and available. It is also important for the Christian to know that God breathed His power on these people only when they had become committed to His will. When God's power comes into a person, he asserts it.

John Milton put it this way in *The Reason of Church Government Urged Against Prelaty:*

> To every good and peaceable man it must in nature be a
> hateful thing to be a displeaser and molester of thousands;

much better would it like him doubtless to be a messenger
of gladness and contentment. . . . But when God commands
to take the trumpet to blow a dolorous or jarring blast, it
lies not in man's will what he shall say or what he shall
conceal.

**And there appeared unto them cloven tongues like as of fire,
and it sat upon each of them.**

Acts 2:3

Fire is used as an emblem again and again throughout the Bible.
We recall how John the Baptist announced, "I indeed baptize you
with water unto repentance . . . he shall baptize you with the Holy
Ghost and with fire" (Matthew 3:11). Jesus said, "I am come to send
fire on the earth . . ." (Luke 12:49). Fire is a symbol of that which
is both destructive and creative. There is the fire of anger and also
the fire of love. There is the fire of the sunshine which gives life,
and also the fire of the lightning which destroys.

The Pentecostal fire is a warming, creative experience. We speak
of one being "set on fire for God." Coldness and indifference is
burned away, enthusiasm takes possession of one, the warmth of
love pervades the emotions, our beliefs become living forces. Speaking of a football team, a sportswriter wrote, "The team caught fire
in the second half." We understand that expression. The team
began to execute, to move, to win. The same thing happens when
a church "catches fire," or when even one Christian "catches fire."

Also, fire is a symbol of purity. Isaiah speaks of how the filth of
the people shall be washed away by the "spirit of burning" (*see*
Isaiah 4:4). "Turning over a new leaf," moral reformation, never
takes the sin out of the soul of man. There are only two powers
which can conquer sin—the blood of Christ and the fire of the Holy
Spirit. The fire suggests that not only is sin forgiven, it is "burned
away." The roots of sin are destroyed and it no longer holds any

power over the person. The fire conquers and overcomes.

The fourteenth-century Augustinian priest, author of *The Imitation of Christ,* Thomas à Kempis said that sin is first a simple suggestion, then a strong imagination, then delight, and then assent. When the Holy Spirit fills a human heart, that process is completely reversed. Not only is the assent to sin taken away, also the delight, the imagination and even the suggestion.

The fire came in the form of **tongues.** It was not a shapeless flame. The tongue is the instrument to be used in the establishment of the faith. Man is to speak to his fellow man. Spoken words shall transmit God's truth. The Kingdom shall spread by the process of people telling other people. "Ye shall be witnesses unto me" (Acts 1:8). A witness is one who tells what he knows. A Christian is one who keeps the faith but does not keep it to himself. ". . . Woe is unto me, if I preach not the gospel!" cried Saint Paul (1 Corinthians 9:16).

Notice—the tongue of fire "sat upon **each** of them." John saw it on Peter; Andrew saw it on Nathaniel; James saw it on Mary; and on around the entire group. No one was left out. Each was given a witness of his own. It came not only upon the Lord's twelve chosen apostles; not only upon the seventy who had been commissioned as evangelists; but upon every believer. The ongues of fire were just as real on the heads of those present whose name we have never heard, as it was upon the head of John, the beloved disciple. It made each and every one of them a priest of God, and so does even to this very day. Each one of us is called, in the words of the folk hymn:

> Go tell it on the mountain,
> Over the hills and everywhere.

We also note that the fire came upon their **heads.** There has been much emphasis among Christian people upon the heart, the heels and the hands. That is—the emotions, the going and the serving.

These are all important and must not be left out. Neither must the head be left out. We are familiar with the phrase, "head over heels." That phrase points up the task of Christian education. A Christian must always remember to "Study to shew thyself approved unto God, a workman that needeth not to be ashamed, rightly dividing the word of truth" (2 Timothy 2:15).

And they were all filled with the Holy Spirit. . . .

Acts 2:4 RSV

Now the Spirit, the third person of the Trinity, was fully come. God had come again into His world. This time not as the Creator, not as a baby born in Bethlehem, but as experience within a human being. This is the third coming of the Lord. First God came to create the earth and the things on the earth, including man. He established the laws by which the world operates and by which man must live. Second, God came in the person of Christ as man's Teacher, Saviour, Lord and Friend. Third, God came in the form of the Spirit to fulfill the promise, "Tarry ye until ye be endued with power from on high" (*see* Luke 24:49); "But ye shall receive power, after that the Holy Spirit is come upon you . . ." (Acts 1:8).

This experience is sometimes referred to as the *Baptism of the Spirit,* or the *Second Blessing.* It may come instantaneously or it may come as a growing experience over a period of time. There are many Christians who have become filled with the Spirit who cannot point to one precise moment when it happened. The important thing is not the **how** or the **when** of the experience, it is the **fact** of the power it gives.

We recall the story of the pool of Bethesda in the fifth chapter of John. Around the pool were porches. "In these lay a great multitude of impotent folk . . ." (verse 3). My dictionary defines impotent as "Powerless to act or to accomplish anything; helpless; physically weak; lacking self-control; unrestrained." Lying on the porches of our world today are great multitudes of impotent folk.

Many are unable to cope with the pressures of life and they become nervous, irritable, tense, and afraid. Daily the number of suicides increases. Alcoholism is one of our society's most prevalent diseases. The use of dope in various forms is growing. Loneliness is a problem by which many are overwhelmed. Divorce has become common in many instances because two people are unable to communicate. Lacking inner strengths and resources, numbers and numbers of people are unable to stand up to life.

After the death of Christ, His disciples shut themselves behind doors and trembled with fear (*see* John 20:19). This is certainly not true of the Christian church but the church is not as potent in today's world as it can be and ought to be. In recent years the church has lost influence and thereby is losing numbers. In the face of many of today's problems, the church has not been able to communicate the mind of Christ. Instead of the power to tell effectively the Good News of God, the church has given itself too much to being assembled behind doors.

Those of us who love the church and believe in her ministry and purpose, often feel impotent in our world. Behind our doors we pass resolutions and talk of reorganizations. But we really feel helpless to do much. Some have decried the denominationalism within the Christian church. But go back and study the beginning of each of our denominations and you find it came out of a feeling of strength and power. A group of people had convictions and believed they could do things. Some of the talk of church mergers that we hear today reminds of one leaning tombstones against each other.

After Pentecost, those Christians in the first century got out from behind doors. Their world became aware of both their presence and their power. Today, let us sing:

> Come, Holy Ghost, our hearts inspire,
> Let us Thine influence prove:

Source of the old prophetic fire,
Fountain of life and love.

CHARLES WESLEY

When a person becomes filled with the Spirit, he possesses power. No longer is one a "reed shaken with the wind" (*see* Luke 7:24), that is, a person overwhelmed by every outside influence. Instead, a Spirit-filled person faces whatever there is to face in life and overcome it. Inner resources become stronger than outside pressures.

. . . and began to speak with other tongues . . . .

Acts 2:4

When the Spirit enters into a person, there is an immediate desire for expression. The first and highest expression is one of praise to God. It is not easy to express our deep spiritual experiences in words. Sometimes we just cannot say what is in our hearts. At times we cannot verbally express our feelings. Saint Paul had this in mind when he said, "Likewise the Spirit helps us in our weakness; for we do not know how to pray as we ought, but the Spirit himself intercedes for us with sighs too deep for words" (Romans 8:26 RSV). The *King James Version* puts it, "With groanings which cannot be uttered."

For many people, this is a valid and useful outward expression of an inner spiritual experience. *Speaking in tongues* can be compared to the experience of crying. At times one feels deep hurt or anguish and there are really no words to express the feeling. Yet the feeling demands expression, so God gave to people the ability to cry. As a pastor, I have at times said to someone, "Get alone and have a good cry." It can be therapy—crying is often good for the soul. Laughter is another expression of inner feelings.

Likewise, there are times when one feels compelled to express the ecstasy of the soul which is possessed by the Holy Spirit, yet no words are adequate. This has been called wordless praise. It is both an expression and a release for deep religious emotion. Many testify to the spiritual value of this expression.

There are those who regard *speaking in tongues* to be more than just the outward expressions of inner feelings. They believe that the Holy Spirit speaks to and through a person in a language which the conscious mind does not understand. Instead of it being gibberish or meaningless words, they are the words coming out of the unconscious mind. Even though the words do not sound rational to the conscious mind, they have meaning within the unconscious mind. Perhaps this is what Saint Paul had in mind when he said, "And he who searches the hearts of men knows what is the mind of the Spirit, because the Spirit intercedes for the saints according to the will of God" (Romans 8:27 RSV). Many testify to a real sense of communication with God through the experience of "speaking in tongues."

We do not question the validity of the two above-mentioned experiences for many people. On the other hand, neither do we demand that everyone who is baptized by the Holy Spirit give those same expressions. For many *speaking in tongues* is not an acceptable experience for themselves. We do not deny the experience for some, neither do we demand it for all.

However it is done, the expression of one's spiritual inner feelings must not be the final expression. The expression of inner feelings is good, but it must go further into action. Pentecost resulted in more than an emotional experience—it resulted in changing the wrongs in both the person's life and the person's world.

The experience of the Spirit is not just for our enjoyment. We are baptized with the Spirit not just for our own sake but also for the sake of our neighbor. In his poem "The Everlasting Mercy," John Masefield said it best:

> I know that Christ had given me birth
> To brother all the souls on earth.

On my shelves are volumes of Adam Clarke's *Commentary* on the Bible. I have spent many hours studying the words of that inspired scholar of some two hundred years ago. In Westminster Abbey, I felt deeply moved as I saw the candle on his tomb and the words inscribed there, "In burning for others, I myself, also, have been consumed."

In this connection, we are reminded of the story we have heard many times of the man who hurried to the church door one Sunday noon and said, "Is the service over?" An usher replied, "The worship is over, but the service is only beginning."

There are some whose hearts are deeply inspired through a stately, formal worship service—a service when the ancient creeds are spoken with reverence, when the prayers are read in words that are lofty and dignified, when the music is the best of such as Beethoven or Bach. Others find joy and inspiration in a much more informal service of worship. They like to sing the gospel hymns, to hear the word proclaimed with fervor, and to have *Amen*s and *Hallelujah*s come from the pews. Some like to spend long hours in a service where there is shouting and weeping.

But we must never forget, whatever tongues are used in the expression of our faith, this faith must be expressed in life and in action.

To speak with other tongues has other significance. God had said through the prophet Joel, "I will pour out of my Spirit upon all flesh" (*see* Joel 2:28 and Acts 2:17). The Word of God this day ceased to be confined to just one language and just one people. This day the Jewish mold was forever broken. God further said through Joel, "Whosoever shall call on the name of the Lord shall be saved" (*see* Joel 2:32 and Acts 2:21). In that moment the Word of God truly became a world language.

On the day of Pentecost the Word of God was heard in perhaps a dozen languages. Centuries later, Charles Wesley prayed:

> O for a thousand tongues to sing
> My great Redeemer's praise

and today his prayer has been answered many times over.

God is the God of all people—whoever and wherever they are. From that day, Christians have not only recognized that all peoples have a right to the Good News of God—Christians have also felt compelled to carry that News to all people. The right of people to hear coupled with it the obligation to proclaim it.

As they began to speak with other tongues, we see the beginning of the fulfilling of their commission. "Go ye therefore, and teach all nations . . ." (Matthew 28:19). "Ye shall be witnesses unto me both in Jerusalem . . . and unto the uttermost part of the earth" (Acts 1:8). The Christian faith was a begin-at-home religion but not a stay-at-home religion. Jesus did not heal the last person in one town before he healed the first person in the next town.

Notice further, "they were all filled . . . and began to speak." The testimony was not reserved to just a select few. Peter preached that day, but so did all the others speak. The preacher stands in the pulpit but every member of the church has both obligation and opportunity to tell it to others. I once asked a large number of new members what first brought them to this church. Several answers were given—newspaper advertising, hearing the services on radio and television, the reputation of the minister—but the largest number said, "I came to this church because of a personal invitation by one of the members." **Every** Christian must speak.

One further thought—"Every man heard—in his own language." The Christian message applies to every condition of mankind, it meets every need of every person. The preacher looks out upon his congregation and he sees youth who are eager to go out in quest of the world. Also, he sees those who are aged and are looking toward that "land that is fairer than day!" There are the lonely, those under the burden of guilt, many who are overwhelmed by the pressures of life, many who are carrying a deep sorrow, those who are struggling with some hard decision. Each hears the Gospel of Christ at the point of his own need and it is sufficient.

... **you shall be baptized with the holy spirit.**

Acts 1:5 RSV

The promise of the Baptism of the Spirit was to those first Christians—it is *no less* a promise to a Christian today. How can one receive this Baptism? The answer is: the conditions are the same now as they were at the beginning.

First, they committed their lives. Before the Lord said, "Tarry ye until ye be endued with power," He said, "Ye are witnesses" (*see* Luke 24:48,49). God never gives power until one is first committed to a purpose. Too often people only think of salvation in terms of the forgiveness of past sins. Salvation also looks to the life to be lived. Salvation is both **from** something and **to** something. The term "good for nothing" is really a contradiction in terms. Goodness is always *for* something. God never gives power to a person who will not use it.

Second, they believed the promise of "... the Holy Spirit, whom the Father will send in my name" (John 14:26 RSV). Before His death, Jesus told the disciples He would live again. "Yet a little while, and the world will see me no more, but ye will see me . . ." (John 14:19 RSV). They did not believe and thus they did not look for Him. Instead, they ran away to hide in fear—"the doors were shut where the disciples were assembled for fear" (*see* John 20:19). They were not thinking of carrying on His work. Instead, they were thinking in terms of trying to get into their old lives again. "Simon Peter saith unto them, I go a fishing. They said unto him, We also go with thee . . ." (John 21:3).

As they were assembled in that upper room, there was no talk of going back. There was no doubting that the Spirit would come. We recall that Saint Paul said to the jailor, "Believe on the Lord Jesus Christ, and thou shalt be saved, and thy house" (Acts 16:31). Belief precedes salvation. "But without faith it is impossible to please him: for he that cometh to God must believe that he is, and that he is a rewarder of them that diligently seek him"

(Hebrews 11:6). Faith precedes experience.

Third, they prayed for the Spirit to come. "These all continued with one accord in prayer . . ." (Acts 1:14). Their prayer was not a device to persuade God to do something, but rather was it a preparation which enabled God to do something. There are many gifts which God gives to us, whether we ask for them or not—the sunshine and the rain, the air we breathe, and on and on. But there are some gifts God cannot give until we ask for them. A father gives his child a house in which to live, clothes to wear and food to eat. Whether the child asks for these things or not, they are provided. But a father cannot give his child an education unless the child asks for it. To ask is the expression of need and desire. As they prayed in that upper room, their hearts became prepared to receive.

Fourth, they waited. "Tarry ye until ye be endued" (*see* Luke 24:49). They were promised that the power on high would come, but they were not promised when it would come. Suppose they had said to each other, "Jesus promised that we would be baptized by the Holy Spirit; we believe that promise; let's gather together and pray for it." So far so good. But suppose after two or three hours of prayer, they had asked each other, "Have you received it?" and each answered, "No," and then they had said, "There is nothing going to happen, let's give up." Of course, nothing would ever have happened.

Why did God delay sending the Spirit? It may have been that God had to wait until they were ready to receive it. It may have been that God waited until conditions in the city were right. As a result of Pentecost, that very day "about three thousand souls" (*see* Acts 2:41) were added to their number. Maybe if it had happened the day before, the people would not have been gathered there. It is for God to decide the *when*.

So it is with each of us. If any one of us keeps committed, keeps believing, and keeps praying, he can be sure that at the proper time, God's power will come into our lives. We must remember, "And let us not be weary in well doing: for in due season we shall reap, if we faint not" (Galatians 6:9).

3

The Results of the Coming of the Holy Spirit

As we follow the lives of those first Christians, we see the results which came from the coming of the Holy Spirit.

And the multitude of them that believed were of one heart and of one soul . . . .

Acts 4:32

Put a tray of ice cubes into a vessel. At first, each cube is separate from the others. But as they begin to warm up, they melt together into one piece. This typifies what happened at Pentecost.

The oneness of His followers was a chief concern of Jesus. He told them, "By this shall all men know that ye are my disciples, if ye have loved one to another" (John 13:35). But the disciples quarrelled among themselves as who would occupy the chief seats. They were jealous of each other. Even at the Last Supper, each felt too big and important to serve the others. At the Last Supper, the Lord Himself had to assume the role of servant and wash their feet.

When the Spirit came upon them, they became "of one heart and of one soul." Then they became united into an unbroken fellowship. This oneness not only included the twelve, it included the hundred and twenty, and it went far beyond them. Included also were Samaritans and Gentiles; people of Jerusalem and people of every other land. From that day, Christian brotherhood transcended all the barriers of man—national, racial, and social.

Not only did they love each other, they loved everybody. As Stephen was being stoned to death, he prayed, "Lord, lay not this sin to their charge" (Acts 7:60). This marked him as a close kinsman of Him who said, "Father, forgive them; for they know not what they do" (Luke 23:34). When the Holy Spirit comes into a heart, there is no room for hate, resentment, prejudice, or anger.

They had all things in common.

Acts 2:44

They went out and sold everything they had and brought what they received and laid it on the altar of the Lord (*see* Acts 2:45). I do not believe that being a Christian means that I sell everything I have and give it to God's work. But I do believe that a Christian is willing to do that, if he believes God wants him to do it. A Christian puts his relationship to God above his material possessions.

I can think of many instances of giving after the Spirit of God had entered into a heart. Here I tell of one experience. The church of which I was pastor needed to build a sanctuary. I preached that Sunday about giving. After the service a man came and handed me five ten-dollar bills. He told me that he had been saving all during the summer to buy himself a winter suit. But he had decided that instead he wanted to give what he had saved to help build the church. All that winter that man came to church wearing a light-colored, thin summer suit. I suppose some people wondered why he would wear a summer suit during the cold days of winter. But each Sunday as I saw him in his place, I felt he was the best-dressed man in the church.

If one wishes to read the heights and depths of the Christian faith, read a handful of pledge cards in the church. Some pledges are so shot through with the Spirit of the Cross, they gladden your heart. Some are so cheap and little, they make you ashamed.

It has been often said that when people get the Spirit, they will give. Also, the reverse is true—when people start giving, they will get the Spirit.

. . . they spoke the word of God with boldness.

Acts 4:31

Not many weeks before, when Simon Peter was accused of being a friend of Jesus, he declared, "I know him not" (*see* Luke 22:57). Not one of Christ's disciples spoke in His behalf during His trials and Crucifixion. But on the day of Pentecost, when they were being ridiculed, "Peter, standing up with the eleven, lifted up his voice . . ." (Acts 2:14). From that day on, they never hesitated to speak the name of Jesus. When they were commanded not to speak or teach in the name of Jesus, their reply was, "For we cannot but speak the things which we have seen and heard" (Acts 4:20). They became both a "fellowship of the unashamed" and also a "fellowship of the unafraid."

There are so many ways to witness for Christ—preaching in the pulpit, teaching a class, singing in the choir, sharing with other people. In this connection we think of the eleven who stood up with Peter. They were willing to let him do the speaking, but standing with him, they gave him the support to make his speaking so much more effective. I heard of a deaf man who faithfully attended church every Sunday. When asked why he came though unable to hear anything that was said, he replied, "I go to let people know whose side I am on."

There are people everywhere with empty hearts and empty lives, who would eagerly respond to someone telling them of his own faith. There are many who would quickly respond to an invitation to become a part of some Christian fellowship. More people than we might suspect are wanting someone to speak the Word to them.

There is another side to witnessing. Dwight L. Moody was

quoted as saying, "I speak to some person every day about Christ. Even if that person does not respond, it keeps my own heart warm!"

. . . These men are full of new wine.

Acts 2:13

The coming of the Holy Spirit gave to these Christians a new optimism and joy. They became so excited and happy that those who saw them thought they were drunk. We have been to football games and have seen a stadium full of people who rise to their feet, clap their hands, and shout at the top of their voices. We have seen the same things happen after a performance by a great symphony orchestra.

While I was a seminary student I served as pastor of a small church. On my way back to school I would often stop in a certain church for the last half of the service there. The preacher there was a powerful man and his sermons often stirred the people mightily. I remember one Sunday when a lady at the close of the sermon stood up and said in a loud voice, "I am so happy my cup runneth over." A lady across the aisle jumped up and cried, "I am so happy my cup runneth over—and my saucer, too." When religion fails to make people happy and excited, it loses much of its appeal.

The Pentecostal joy, however, was much more than mere emotion. It was a joy of confidence, of newfound strength, of optimistic faith. These people in that upper room had seen their Lord crucified. They lived under the heavy hand of a dictatorship. Their entire world was in opposition to them. But with the power of the Holy Spirit within them, they believed they could win.

Their optimism was justified. Suppose somebody had looked at that small group of happy Christians and said, "Those people will shake cities. They will change the course of human history. They will be like the rising sun, bringing light and warmth to the world.

Their work will go on for centuries and centuries, and millions upon countless millions of lives will be influenced by them." Such a comment on the day of Pentecost would have been scoffed at. Yet that and far more has happened. No one would have dreamed that this movement called Christianity would have outlasted the mighty Roman empire. Yet we sing:

> O where are kings and empires now,
> Of old that went and came?
> But Lord, Thy Church is praying yet,
> A thousand years the same.

A. CLEVELAND COXE

Every church has well-meaning people who are quick to say about any forward step, such things as, "It is a good idea but we cannot put it over," and "Now is not the time, let us wait until next year." But when a person becomes conscious of inner resources, then is optimism born. The Spirit of God and the spirit of defeat just cannot live together in the same heart.

. . . great grace was upon them all.

Acts 4:33

One of the favorite words of the early Christians was *grace*. It appears no less than ninety-five times in the writing of Saint Paul. There are three meanings of grace in the Bible. "By grace ye are saved" (*see* Ephesians 2:5). Here the meaning is unmerited favor, loving kindness, the mercy of God. Thus we sing:

> Amazing grace! How sweet the sound,
> That saved a wretch like me!

JOHN NEWTON

"My grace is sufficient for thee . . ." (2 Corinthians 12:9). Paul had a "thorn in the flesh." He asked God to remove it. Instead God gave him the grace to bear it. Here grace means strength and power to overcome (*see* verses 7–10).

"Great grace was upon them all." Across many years, one of my favorite places has been the Highlands (North Carolina) Country Club. Late in the afternoon I like to sit on the big porch there. The setting sun seems like a halo on the mountain peaks. A reverent quiet descends. The mountains, the trees, the tiny lake, even the rocks cast a magic spell. It seems in that moment that the grace of the Lord comes over the earth. I think of the hymn:

> Drop Thy still dews of quietness,
> Till all our strivings cease;
> Take from our souls the strain and stress,
> And let our ordered lives confess
> The beauty of Thy peace.

JOHN GREENLEAF WHITTIER

The Holy Spirit brings this grace upon the lives of people. Being filled with the Spirit, one begins to live above the petty irritations of life. One develops an undisturbed, calm attitude. Possessing the Spirit, one becomes controlled, not given to anger, to harsh criticisms of others, to fear. Instead, a love for others begins to radiate and, in turn, one becomes easy to love by others. God's grace makes one winsome and attractive.

Once a lady's dainty handkerchief seemed ruined by an ugly ink spot. An artist friend asked to borrow that handkerchief and took it home. When he brought it back, where there had been a blot, there now was beauty, for he had made the blot the foundation of a lovely design. God does that with the ugly blots on our lives and in our personalities, as we become filled with His Spirit.

... And the Lord added to the church daily such as should be saved.

Acts 2:47

We recall Ruth saying to Naomi, "Thy God shall be my God" (*see* Ruth 1:16). Ruth did not know Naomi's church; she had gone to another church. She did not even know Naomi's God. Living in Moab, she had worshiped another God. But Ruth knew Naomi. She had seen her when times were hard, when life was monotonous, when sorrow weighed heavily upon her. Day by day, Ruth had lived with Naomi and she was saying, "I want the religion that can make me like you."

As the pastor of a church, I have long known that people do not remember the sermons I preach. One can go to some church I have served and say to people there, "Tell me some of the sermons Charles Allen preached here." A few might be able to name one or two sermons. But ask those same people, "Do you remember the life Charles Allen lived? Was it a good life? Was he kind and loving? Did he put God first?" The people can answer those questions. They remember how the preacher lived, long after they have forgotten what he said.

So it is in the church. We can build beautiful buildings, give ourselves to social actions and do all the things that Christians should do. But above all, people are attracted to Christ by the lives of those who profess Christ. These first Christians lived in such a way that, wherever they went, others saw them and said, "I want to be one of you."

4

The Fruit of the Spirit

But the fruit of the Spirit is love, joy, peace, longsuffering, gentleness, goodness, faith, meekness, temperance. . . .

Galatians 5:22, 23

In the Sermon on the Mount, our Lord is speaking about both trees and people when He says, "Wherefore by their fruits ye shall know them" (Matthew 7:20). The real test of whether or not the Holy Spirit dwells in a person is the life that is produced. Saint Paul lists nine qualities of character which the Spirit-filled life possesses.

Love

Once I was preaching in a revival in a small rural church. In one of the morning services, I invited people to give their own testimony, to tell what the Lord had done in their own lives. I shall never forget one man in particular. He had spent his life working a small farm. He was not educated in a formal way, but he gave one of the best descriptions of Christian love I have ever heard.

He stood and said, "When I was a little boy I loved my mother. As I grew older I felt I would never love anybody else but my mother. As a young man I met a girl and I came to love her and I married her. I then loved my mother and my wife but I knew I would never love anyone else. Then a baby boy was born into our home. As I held him in my arms, I knew that I loved him, too. We

55

never had any other children and those were the only three people I loved. Then during a service here in this church, the Lord Jesus came into my heart. When I came to know Jesus as my Saviour, I loved Him. Then a strange thing happened. Loving my mother and my wife and my son did not cause me to love anybody else. But when I loved Jesus, *then I loved everybody!*"

I have read many books of the scholars, but not anyone has said it better than that simple man. One person can love another person and it can end there. When one begins to love the Lord, there is no end to that love. When the Spirit of God dwells in a life, we do love Him and also we love our fellow men. Christians love family, friends, and even strangers they chance to meet. Christians love those of their community and also their world; those of their race and also of every other race. The Holy Spirit makes it possible for a person to do what Jesus said: "Love your enemies, bless them that curse you, do good to them that hate you, and pray for them which despitefully use you, and persecute you" (Matthew 5:44).

The fruit of the Spirit is love—love for God and mankind.

Joy

In a sermon, I said, "Jesus was the most joyful person who ever lived." Afterward a friend took me to task, saying "Jesus was not joyful, He was a 'man of sorrows and acquainted with grief' (*see* Isaiah 53:3)." But we must know that joy and sorrow are not contradictory words. Jesus did experience sorrow—and disappointment—and pain—and frustration—and loneliness. But listen to His own words: "These things have I spoken unto you, that my joy might remain in you, and that your joy might be full" (John 15:11).

Just as all the water in the world cannot quench the fire of the Holy Spirit, neither can all the troubles and tragedies of the world overwhelm the joy which the Spirit brings into the human heart. There is a Cross at the heart of the Christian faith, but that does not alter the fact that there is joy in the heart of the Christian. On the day of Pentecost, observers thought that the Christians were drunk. Instead they were filled with such joy they could not contain themselves.

Sometimes we confuse joy and pleasure. Pleasure depends on circumstances and pleasures can come and go. What brings pleasure today may not bring it tomorrow. But joy is an experience that does not come and go. It is deep and real. Jesus said to His disciples, ". . . In the world ye shall have tribulation; but be of good cheer: I have overcome the world" (John 16:33). In spite of what happens, the Christian has optimistic faith in God's triumph. The Christian even looks at death and sees eternal joy beyond.

The basic enemies of joy are worry, guilt, and the fear of defeat. When one rejoices in the Lord, worries are overcome, forgiveness is a real experience, and one possesses the assurance that God's cause will triumph.

Peace

Jesus said to His followers, "My peace I give unto you" (*see* John 14:27). Saint Paul prayed, "Now the God of peace be with you all" (Romans 15:33). "The fruit of the Spirit is peace." There are some things this peace is not. It does not mean indifference to the world. One can be deeply concerned about the tragedies and injustices of life, and even be at war against evil, yet still possess inward peace.

Jeremiah exclaimed, "Oh that I had in the wilderness a lodging place of wayfaring men that I might leave my people . . ." (Jeremiah 9:2). Sometimes he got fed up with people and just wanted to get away. We sometimes have that feeling. But getting away from it all is not peace. One could spend the remainder of life on a desert island alone and still not have peace. People seek to isolate themselves in many different ways—for instance, living behind closed doors. Jesus spoke about entering into a closet, closing the door and praying (*see* Matthew 6:6). But He did not intend that one should live all the time in a closet with the door shut. In the church we have groups that give themselves to quiet times and retreats, but just "stillness" is not peace.

Self-righteousness can be a form of escapism, as can daydreams and fantasies. Many have the idea that they could be at peace if only the circumstances of their lives were different—a home in a better neighborhood, enough wealth for financial security, a different job, and on and on.

Peace is a positive gift of God "which passeth all understanding" (*see* Philippians 4:7). Those first Christians met toil, suffering, and death. They gave themselves completely to their tasks and never ran away, but they never ceased to possess peace. When one believes in God and is wholly committed to God's will, all the enemies of peace are overcome. The moment I begin to really love any person, I am at peace with that person in my heart. Peace comes because of the indwelling of the Spirit and in spite of any condition of life which we are called upon to face.

Long-Suffering

Other translations here use the word "patience" and perhaps that word is better. However, it is needful that we be reminded that the Holy Spirit is not a buffer against suffering. "Why has this happened to me?" is a question on many lips. We can think of suffering as a sign that God does not love us or that He has forgotten us. We can give ourselves to complaining, to self-pity, to bitterness, and to a "get-even" spirit. Suffering can be deeply resented.

On the other hand, one can actually be falsely proud of suffering. Some see suffering as a mark of their piety and enjoy telling about it to whomever will listen. In fact, the more it is told, the larger it becomes in one's mind. "But God forbid that I should glory, save in the cross of our Lord Jesus Christ . . ." (Galatians 6:14), said Saint Paul. He did not say we should glory in our own crosses. One of our subtle temptations is to brag about our troubles and sufferings.

The Holy Spirit gives the power to bear with patience whatever hurts that life may bring. Patience can live today while it waits for tomorrow. It is not mere resignation, but rather is it enduring courage. Jeremiah suffered in so many ways. Not only did he know physical pain, he knew all the frustrations of a prophet. Out of his sufferings, he came to the point where he could say, "It is good that a man should both hope and quietly wait for the salvation of the Lord" (Lamentations 3:26). We may be in a hurry, but God may not be in a hurry. Patience comes of learning this.

Long-suffering—patience—also comes out of the conviction that the only real sorrow is a wasted sorrow. Every grief has a lesson to teach, every sorrow has a gift to give, every suffering has a reason. The Christian believes that God always has a next step for His children to take. The Cross is never God's last word. One can believe that suffering is a price one pays for something that is very much worth that price. It may be a time until one realizes what that something is, but the Spirit gives one patience—the strength to suffer long.

Gentleness

Both the *Revised Standard Version* and the *New English Bible* use the word "kindness." In the New Testament, the Greek word used means "a kindly disposition," or "a gentle spirit." It does not so much refer to actions as it does to an attitude. We use such expressions as "a kind spirit" or "a gentle soul." Some tend to confuse this attitude with spinelessness. Kindness or gentleness is really a very strong trait of character.

Unkindness, paradoxically, is one of the first sins of religious people. When one reaches a self-satisfactory spiritual level, there is a temptation to be proud of the accomplishment. At the same time, one may become very unsympathetic with those who have not attained such a state. In one's disdain of sin, one can be harsh and unkind toward a sinner. We recall that Jesus never spoke an unkind word to any sinner. Yet He spoke some harsh words to certain religious people. He said to some, "O generations of vipers" (*see* Matthew 3:7) and also, "O ye hypocrites" (*see* Matthew 16:3). Some people seem to have such a passion for righteousness that they have no room left for compassion for those who have failed.

Look back into your own life and think of those who have helped and influenced you the most. Think of your teachers, ministers, and various people in the community. Isn't it true that those who were kind and gentle in manner and spirit are the names you write first? We have reason to believe that the Gospel of Christ would have a much larger hold on the world today, if only those who preach it were a little more gentle in their attitudes.

Also, kindness is a powerful force. Perhaps Albert Schweitzer said it best in *Memoirs of Childhood and Youth:*

> All ordinary violence produces its own limitations, for it calls forth an answering violence which sooner or later becomes its equal or superior. But kindness works simply and perseveringly; it produces no strained relations which prejudice its working, strained relations which already exist it relaxes. Mistrust and misunderstanding it puts to flight, and it strengthens itself by calling forth answering kindness. Hence it is the furthest reaching and most effective of all forces.

The Spirit softens a harsh personality.

Goodness

Goodness is not the most sought after human trait. The word "goodness" has suffered somewhat the same fate of "A certain man [who] went down from Jerusalem to Jericho, and fell among thieves, which stripped him of his raiment, and wounded him, and departed, leaving him half dead" (Luke 10:30). You may say of a girl, "Mary is beautiful—or talented—or intelligent" and she will feel complimented. But if you simply say, "Mary is a good girl," she will not likely appreciate that.

I have sometimes heard it said of a preacher, "He can't preach but he is a good man." That is not really a compliment. No church ever called a minister just because he is a good man.

My own father was a faithful and effective minister for many years. I admired and appreciated him very much. Once he said to me, "When I die, on the marker at my grave, put my name, the year I was born, and the year I died. Then, if those who know me best can honestly say it, I would like for you to put these words, 'He was a good man.' " I was disappointed because I would want to say something better. But I got interested in that word "good" and I found it literally means "to be like God." No higher compliment can be paid than that.

It was said of Barnabas, "for he was a good man, full of the Holy Spirit and of faith" (Acts 11:24 RSV). The two go together.

Some have confused goodness with mere ethics. They set up their own code as to what is right and wrong and then take pride in their good life. Others adopt the Boy Scout oath to "Do a good turn daily," and proudly tell themselves that they are good. Such goodness leads to self-reverence. Real goodness comes through the indwelling Spirit shining through a person. Ethics and good deeds are but results of goodness.

Faith

This fruit of the Spirit does not refer to one's religious beliefs. Many of us are too concerned about what to believe. Across the centuries, Christians have argued the **whats** of faith. If someone does not exactly agree with our own idea of orthodoxy, we have been too quick to withdraw fellowship. Jesus never said very much about **what**. He said, "Follow me, and I will make you fishers of men" (Matthew 4:19); ". . . take up the cross, and follow me" (Mark 10:21); "And I, if I be lifted up from the earth, will draw all men unto me" (John 12:32). The Christian is concerned with **who**.

This fruit of the Spirit literally means being faithful. It is fidelity. Saint John said to the Christians, ". . . be thou faithful unto death" (Revelation 2:10). That means to be faithful not only until one dies, it also means to be faithful, even if it causes death. The Spirit-filled person would rather die than be unfaithful to the Lord.

In truth, one is required to die to self, in order to achieve complete faithfulness to Christ. As Paul said, "I live, yet not I, but Christ liveth in me" (*see* Galatians 2:20). The Christian has no ambition but Christ's ambition. Self-preservation ceases to be one's concern. This is why a Christian can suffer the loss of anything and everything and not waver. After Pentecost, those first Christians had something beyond themselves to live for. No person ever becomes great until he completely gives himself to something greater than himself.

God does not protect His saints. He lets them live in a world where they can suffer, where their hearts can be broken, where temptations are very real, where one might see his best efforts miserably fail. But because of the indwelling Spirit, none of these has the power to make the Christian unfaithful. "God let my child die, I will never trust Him again," says an anguished mother. We sympathize with her, but we also pray that she may open her heart and life to the Holy Spirit.

Meekness

Here is another virtue which is a subtle temptation of religious people. Remembering that Jesus said, "I am meek and lowly in heart" (*see* Matthew 11:29), one is tempted to feign a lowliness which is not real. Someone said of a certain minister, "Someday he will write a book on *How I Achieved Humility*." Sometimes one outwardly depreciates himself as a method of gaining appreciation. Some use self-effacement as a means of gaining face.

The Christian does not need to practice self-depreciation. God never expects us to be less than we really are. He wants us to develop ourselves, to increase our strengths, to use our abilities. There is no virtue in hiding one's talents in the ground. Self-belittlement is an insult to the God who made us. Meekness comes another way.

I shall never forget the first time I saw a giant Sequoia tree. I stood by that great tree and looked at its massive trunk. I thought about how deeply its roots go into the ground. I looked up and saw its magnificent height. Even though I stood as straight and as tall as I could, I felt small by the side of that great tree. Likewise, when I stand before the Lord and see His greatness, His strength, His goodness, then humility and meekness come naturally and are real. When the Holy Spirit comes into our lives, we cease to become self-centered and become God-centered. Pride comes from looking only at ourselves, meekness comes through looking at God. Meekness is not something to be pretended. It comes naturally to the Spirit-filled life.

Temperance

The last fruit of the Spirit listed is temperance. The *Revised Standard Version* gives the better translation, "self-control." A person is both body and soul and each is constantly seeking to gain mastery over the other. As we study the lives of even the saints, we find that keeping control over the passions and desires of the body is a never-ending struggle. It is a war within and no truce is ever declared. At this point every Christian must remain eternally vigilant.

Saint Paul gave a fearful warning to every one of us when he said, "But I keep under my body, and bring it into subjection: lest that by any means, when I have preached to others, I myself should be a castaway" (I Corinthians 9:27). When John Wesley was a student at Oxford, his mother wrote him, "My dear Son: Remember that anything which increases the authority of the body over the mind is an evil thing." No one has ever given a better definition of temperance or self-control.

Fasting is one discipline that Christians have used through the centuries. But just as an act by itself, fasting has little value. I visited a very sick child in the hospital one night about nine o'clock. The mother was sitting by the bedside. I said, "Did you eat dinner?" She replied, "No." I then asked, "Did you have lunch?"

She again said, "No." Then she said, "I have been so concerned about my child that I actually forgot about being hungry." The Spirit-filled Christian gives first attention to the needs of the soul and, in so doing, the hungers of the body are often completely conquered.

Even for one who has overcome the baser bodily temptations, there are still dangers. In an affluent society, it is so easy to increase our standard of living. Gradually we add luxury to our daily living. We can become increasingly extravagant. Then, without even realizing it, our luxuries become necessities. This is the point where many of us are most intemperate.

God wants His children to have some cake as well as some bread. We know that Jesus both fasted and feasted. He fasted in the wilderness and He feasted with various people. But He was always the master of His body. That is the Christian's challenge and goal.

231.3   276
CLASS   ACC.

Allen
_____
(LAST NAME OF AUTHOR)

The Miracle of the Holy Spirit
_____
(BOOK TITLE)

FIRST UNITED METHODIST
CHURCH LIBRARY
_____
STAMP LIBRARY OWNERSHIP

CODE 4366-03   BROADMAN SUPPLIES
CLS-3   MADE IN U.S.A.